On Breathing

Understanding the Connection Between Breath and Life

A Modern Translation

Adapted for the Contemporary Reader

Aristotle

Translated by Tim Zengerink

Table of Contents

Preface: Message to the Reader. iv

Introduction. 1

Section 1 10

PREFACE

MESSAGE TO THE READER

Dear Reader,

Thank you for choosing this edition; it is more than just a book—you are reading a living thread of humanity's literary heritage.

We'd like to invite you to **gain immediate, unlimited digital & audiobook access** to hundreds of the most treasured literary classics ever written—along with the option to **secure deluxe paperback, hardcover & box set editions at printing cost**. Together, we can **spark a new global literary renaissance** alongside our small, independent publishing house called "The Library of Alexandria."

Thousands of years ago, the Library of Alexandria stood as a beacon of knowledge—until it was lost to history. We aim to reignite that spirit of preservation and discovery right now, in the modern age—only this time, it's accessible to all, in every language and every format.

Picture a world where every timeless classic, novel, poem, or philosophical treatise is not only available to read but also updated for today's readers—modernized, translated into any language or dialect, and ready to enjoy in any format you choose, whether that is in an eBook, audiobook, paperback, or deluxe hardcover & box set version a printing cost.

By joining our movement to **rebuild the modern Library of Alexandria**, you become part of an unprecedented mission to offer:

- **Unlimited Audiobook & eBook Access to the Greatest Classics of All Time**

  Instantly explore thousands of legendary works, from Plato and Shakespeare to Jane Austen and Leo Tolstoy. All are instantly ready to read or listen to, giving you a complete literary universe at your fingertips.

- **Paperback & Deluxe Editions at Printing Costs:**

  Purchase any title in a paperback, deluxe hardbound, or deluxe boxset edition at printing costs, shipped right to your doorstep. Curate your personal library of Alexandria with editions worthy of display—crafted to last, designed to captivate, and delivered straight to your door.

- **Modern translations for Contemporary Readers in all languages and dialects**

  Discover a vast selection of classics reimagined in clear, current language—no more struggling with outdated phrases or obscure references. Next to the original versions, we aim to offer translations in as many languages and dialects as possible.

As we continue our translation efforts and add new languages, readers everywhere can connect with these works as if they were written today. *By bridging linguistic divides, you're contributing to ensuring that these timeless stories become more meaningful, accessible, and inspiring for people across the globe.*

- **Your Personal Library of Alexandria:**

  Over the months and years, you'll curate a unique physical archive of classics—each volume a testament to your taste, curiosity, and love of knowledge. It's not just about owning books—it's about curating a cultural legacy you'll cherish and pass down for generations to come.

- **Join a Global Literary Renaissance:**

  Your support fuels an ongoing mission: allowing us to reinvest in offering deluxe print editions (including special boxsets) at their true cost, broaden the range of available formats and translations, and extend the reach of these works to new audiences worldwide. By joining today, you're not just preserving a legacy of masterpieces; *you set in motion a powerful wave of literary accessibility.*

We are more than a publisher—we're a movement, and we can't do it alone. Your support lets us scale our mission, preserving and reimagining history's greatest works for tomorrow's readers.

Become a Torchbearer of knowledge.

Thank you for picking up this book and allowing us into your literary journey. As you turn the pages, know that you're part of something larger: a global effort to keep these stories alive, share their wisdom across borders and generations, and spark a true cultural revival for the modern era.

If this resonates with you—please consider taking the next step. By visiting:
www.libraryofalexandria.com

With gratitude and a shared love of knowledge,

The Modern Library of Alexandria Team

Visit:

www.libraryofalexandria.com

Or scan the code below:

Introduction

Ancient Greece was a civilization famous for its great contributions to philosophy, politics, art, and science. It thrived from the 8th century BCE until the Roman Empire started to decline. Greece's city-states, especially Athens, were the heart of culture and intellectual thought. This was the time when democracy began, impressive buildings like the Parthenon were built, and famous playwrights like Sophocles and Euripides produced their works. The Greeks' curiosity about the world around them laid the foundation for Western philosophy. Thinkers like Socrates, Plato, and later Aristotle, pushed the limits of what people understood about the world.

Greek society was deeply connected to theism, which focused on a large group of gods and goddesses who were believed to control every part of life. But this system did not prevent people from exploring new ideas. In fact, it coexisted with a growing interest in finding logical explanations for nature and human life. Intellectuals would often debate and discuss these ideas in public places like the Agora. Aristotle grew up in this dynamic environment, learning from earlier philosophers, and later challenging and expanding their ideas.

Aristotle's Life

Aristotle was born in 384 BCE in a small town called Stagira, located in northern Greece. His father, Nicomachus, was a doctor for King Amyntas of Macedon, and this allowed Aristotle to be around the Macedonian royal court from a young age. When his parents passed away, Aristotle was sent to Athens at the age of 17 to pursue his education. Athens was the center of intellectual life in Greece, and Aristotle joined Plato's Academy, which was the most respected school of the time. The Academy was a place where students discussed everything from ethics to science. Although Aristotle learned a lot from Plato, he did not always agree with him, especially when it came to metaphysics, which deals with the nature of reality.

After spending almost 20 years at the Academy, Aristotle left Athens around 347 BCE after Plato's death. He traveled around different cities in Greece, continuing to study and learn. In 343 BCE, he was invited to the court of King Philip II of Macedon, where he became the tutor of Philip's son, Alexander, who would later become known as Alexander the Great. Aristotle taught Alexander about philosophy, ethics, politics, and science. Aristotle's influence is visible in Alexander's leadership style, which showed respect for knowledge and strategic thinking.

After teaching Alexander, Aristotle returned to Athens in 335 BCE, where he opened his own school called the Lyceum. Unlike Plato's Academy, the Lyceum focused more on recording knowledge and observing nature. Aristotle and his students performed research, studied animals, and took notes on what they observed. The Lyceum became a major center of learning, and it rivaled Plato's Academy. This is also where Aristotle wrote many of his famous works.

Later in life, after the death of Alexander in 323 BCE, the political climate in Athens became difficult for Aristotle because of his connections to the Macedonian court. Accused of disrespecting the gods, Aristotle decided to leave Athens. He fled to Chalcis, where he passed away in 322 BCE. Even though he had to leave Athens, his legacy lived on through his many writings and the influence of his school, the Lyceum.

Aristotle's Impact on Western Thought

No figure looms larger over the development of Western philosophy and science than Aristotle. A student of Plato and tutor to Alexander the Great, he unified logic, ethics, politics, rhetoric, and metaphysics into a coherent system that shaped intellectual inquiry for centuries. Although his writings reflect the best knowledge of his era, they also reveal a distinctive way of understanding the world—one that balances observation with rigorous logical analysis. Over time, this method has profoundly influenced everything from political theory to modern scientific methodology.

Aristotle approached knowledge as an interconnected whole, seeing each field of study as a vital path toward truth. While many earlier thinkers focused on abstract concepts, he emphasized direct observation of the natural world. By systematically examining and classifying what he saw, Aristotle laid the groundwork for the empirical methods now central to modern science. Although our understanding of nature has evolved, his legacy endures in today's emphasis on evidence-based research.

Logic: The Foundation of Rational Inquiry

Often hailed as the "father of formal logic," Aristotle introduced a system of reasoning that shaped intellectual discourse for over two millennia. In works like the Organon, he analyzed how valid conclusions are drawn from premises and introduced syllogisms—deductive arguments that became standard tools in philosophy, theology, and science. Even contemporary logic, despite its modern mathematical and symbolic advancements, can trace many of its core principles back to Aristotle's pioneering analyses.

Metaphysics: Exploring the Nature of Reality

Aristotle's Metaphysics offered one of the earliest comprehensive explorations of existence at its most fundamental level. There, he described the nature of "being qua being" and introduced the concepts of potentiality and actuality to explain how things change and develop. These ideas deeply influenced medieval scholastics—both Christian and Islamic—who integrated Aristotelian reasoning into their theological frameworks. Today, discussions about consciousness, identity, and free will still reference these Aristotelian notions.

Ethics and the Pursuit of the Good Life

In the Nicomachean Ethics, Aristotle proposed that the ultimate aim of human life is eudaimonia, often translated as "happiness" or "flourishing." He argued that we achieve this through virtue, developed by cultivating good habits guided by reason. His famous Doctrine of the Mean asserts that moral virtue resides between two extremes—for instance, courage lies between recklessness and cowardice. This focus on character formation has profoundly shaped the tradition known as "virtue ethics," influencing modern debates on moral education, personal development, and what it means to live well.

Politics: The Role of the Individual in the City-State

Aristotle's practical approach to ethics naturally extended into political theory. In Politics, he explored various forms of government—monarchy, aristocracy, oligarchy, democracy—and weighed their merits and pitfalls. For Aristotle, a well-ordered polis (city-state) exists not merely for survival or trade but to enable its citizens to live virtuous, fulfilling lives. His conviction that ethics and politics are intertwined remains influential, informing contemporary discussions on citizenship, governance, and justice.

Rhetoric: The Art of Persuasion

In his treatise Rhetoric, Aristotle examined how persuasion works, detailing how arguments must appeal to ethos (credibility), pathos (emotion), and logos (logic). This clear framework for effective communication continues to guide public speakers, legal advocates, and writers. From ancient courtroom orations to modern political campaigns, Aristotelian rhetoric underpins many of the strategies people use to sway audiences and shape public opinion.

Beyond these core subjects, Aristotle made significant contributions to biology, physics, psychology, and aesthetics. In the Poetics, for example, he investigated why humans respond so powerfully to tragic drama, pioneering the concept of catharsis— the emotional release that audiences feel through art. Throughout the medieval period, thinkers like Thomas Aquinas integrated Aristotle's theories into Christian theology, while Islamic philosophers such as Avicenna and Averroes preserved, interpreted, and expanded upon his works.

Across centuries of reinterpretation and debate, Aristotle remains a living voice in contemporary thought. His insistence on systematically gathering evidence and connecting it to logical principles laid the foundation for what we now recognize as the scientific method. His inquiries into human flourishing, civic responsibility, and the nature of argument continue to spark discussion and inspire new research. From personal ethics to societal organization, Aristotle's ideas help us frame enduring questions about how best to live, learn, and understand reality.

In sum, Aristotle stands as a foundational pillar of Western thought. He bridged abstract theorizing and practical inquiry, bequeathing a vision of knowledge that values both reason and experience. From ethics and politics to science and art, his ideas have been woven into countless intellectual traditions. Even today, as we grapple with questions of morality, governance, and truth, we walk in the footsteps of an ancient thinker whose breadth of insight and depth of analysis continue to guide our pursuit of wisdom.

Final Thoughts

By preserving Aristotle's legacy, we protect the intellectual depth and rigor that defined his way of understanding the world. His systematic way of asking questions, his classification of knowledge, and his ethical theories are still relevant today, providing a model for critical thinking across many subjects. This preservation is important not just for philosophy students but for anyone interested in the foundations of human thought and the development of ideas that shape the world we live in.

One of the difficulties in studying Aristotle's work is that his ideas and language are complex. Translating these works into our modern language is a key step in making his profound insights easier for more people to understand. By putting his ideas into today's language, more readers can engage with his thoughts, even if they don't have a background in classical studies. Making Aristotle's work accessible means adapting them to modern ways of thinking without losing their original depth. This helps bridge the gap between ancient and modern readers, making sure Aristotle's work stays relevant.

Section 1

We have already mentioned that life and the presence of a soul involve a certain warmth. Even the process of digesting food, which provides nutrition for animals, doesn't happen without the soul and warmth, because in all cases, digestion is due to heat. That's why the main part of the soul responsible for nutrition must be located in the part of the body where this principle is active. This part is between where food enters and where waste is expelled. In animals without blood, this part doesn't have a name, but in animals with blood, it's called the heart. The blood provides the nourishment from which the animal's organs are made. So, the blood vessels must have the same starting point since they exist to support the blood by serving as its containers. In animals with blood, the heart is where the veins start; they don't pass through it, but instead, they spread out from it, as we can see when we study dissections.

Other abilities of the soul can't exist without the power of nutrition (as explained in the treatise *On the Soul*), and this power depends on natural heat, which Nature has activated by bringing it to life. But fire, as we have already said, can be destroyed in two ways—by going out or burning out. It can be put out by its opposite forces. So, fire can be extinguished by surrounding cold, whether it's in large amounts or spread out (though it happens faster when spread out). This kind of destruction happens by force both in living and non-living things, for cutting an animal apart or freezing it with extreme cold causes death. However, burning out happens when there is too much heat; if the heat is too intense and nothing adds new fuel, the fire will go out because it burns out, not because of cold. So, if it's going to keep going, it needs to be cooled down because cold prevents this kind of burnout.

Some animals live in water, while others live on land. For very small, bloodless animals, the cooling effect of the surrounding water or air is enough to prevent them from burning out due to heat. Since they don't have much heat, they don't need much cold to keep them balanced. This also explains why these animals don't live long, because being small means they have less ability to resist extremes. But some insects live longer, even though they are bloodless like the others, and they have a deep indentation below their middle section to allow cooling through a thinner membrane. These insects are warmer and need more cooling, like bees (some of which live for seven years) and all insects that make a humming noise, such as wasps, beetles, and crickets. They make a sound that's like panting by using air, as the air inside them causes a rising and falling movement that creates friction against the membrane. The way they move this area is similar to how the lungs move in animals that breathe, or how gills move in fish. What happens is like when an animal that breathes air is suffocated by blocking its mouth, causing the lungs to make a similar rising and falling movement. In these animals, this internal movement isn't enough for cooling, but in insects, it is. By creating friction against the membrane, they make the humming sound, as we said, similar to how children make sounds by blowing through a reed covered by a thin membrane. This is also how crickets make their songs; they have more heat and a deeper indentation at the waist, while those that don't make noise have no such indentation.

Animals that have blood and lungs, but whose lungs have little blood and are spongy, can sometimes live for a long time without breathing, because the lung, with its small amount of blood or liquid, can rise very high, and its own movement can keep cooling the body for a long time. But eventually, this is not enough, and the animal dies from suffocation if it doesn't breathe, as we've already mentioned. Exhaustion due to a lack of cooling is called suffocation, and anything that dies this way is said to be suffocated.

We've already said that insects don't breathe like other animals, and we can observe this in small creatures like flies and bees, which can move around in a liquid for a long time as long as it's not too hot or cold. However, animals with little strength tend to breathe more often. These animals die from what we call suffocation when their stomach fills up and the heat in their middle part is lost. This is also why they can revive after being in ashes for some time.

Among water animals, those without blood can live longer in air than those with blood, like fish. Since they have a small amount of heat, the air can cool them for a long time, as we see in animals like crabs and octopuses. However, the air is not enough to keep them alive because they don't have enough heat. Many fish can also live in the soil, though they stay still, and they can be found by digging. All animals that don't have lungs or have bloodless lungs need less cooling.

Regarding bloodless animals, we've explained that some rely on the surrounding air and others on fluids to maintain life. But for animals with blood and a heart, all those with lungs take in air and cool themselves by breathing in and out. All animals that give birth to live young and do so inside their bodies (unlike the Selachia, which give birth outside) have lungs, as do oviparous animals, such as birds and scaly animals like tortoises, lizards, and snakes. In the first group, the lungs are filled with blood, but in most of the latter, the lungs are spongy. So, they breathe less often, as we've said before. This function is also found in animals that live in water, like water snakes, frogs, crocodiles, and turtles, whether they live in the sea or on land, as well as in seals.

All these animals give birth on land and sleep on land, or when they sleep in water, they keep their heads above the surface to breathe. But animals with gills cool themselves by taking in water; this includes Selachia and other animals without legs. Fish have no legs, and their fins are named for their resemblance to wings. However, one animal with legs, the tadpole, has gills.

No animal has both lungs and gills, and the reason is that lungs are made for cooling through air (their name, "pneumon," seems to come from their function as a container for breath), while gills are for cooling through water. Since one tool is enough for one purpose, Nature doesn't make unnecessary organs. So, some animals have gills, others have lungs, but none have both.

Every animal needs food to live and cooling to prevent death. Nature uses the same organ for both tasks. For example, in some animals, the tongue is used both to taste food and for speaking. In animals with lungs, the mouth is used to break down food and to let air in and out. In animals without lungs or that don't breathe, the mouth is just used to break down food, while in animals that need cooling, gills are made for this purpose.

We'll explain later how these organs produce cooling. But to make sure food doesn't interfere with breathing, both respiring animals and those that take in water have a similar system. When they breathe, they don't take in food, because food, whether liquid or dry, could get into the windpipe and cause suffocation by blocking the lungs. The windpipe is located in front of the esophagus, through which food goes into the stomach. In blooded quadrupeds, there is a lid called the epiglottis over the windpipe. In birds and egg-laying quadrupeds, this covering is missing, but they close their windpipes by contracting them. When swallowing food, birds contract the windpipe while mammals close the epiglottis. Once the food has passed, the epiglottis is raised, or the windpipe expands, allowing air to enter and cool the body. In animals with gills, water is expelled first, then food enters the mouth. They don't have a windpipe, so they aren't harmed by liquids entering their windpipe, only by liquids entering the stomach. This is why these animals quickly expel water and grab their food. Their teeth are sharp and often arranged like a saw because they can't chew their food.

Among water animals, cetaceans, like dolphins and whales, may seem puzzling, but they can be explained. Examples of these animals include dolphins, whales, and others with blowholes. They don't have legs but do have lungs, even though they live in water. They have lungs for cooling, as we mentioned, but they don't take in water to cool themselves. Instead, they cool down by breathing because they have lungs. That's why they sleep with their heads out of the water, and dolphins even snore. If they get caught in nets, they die quickly from suffocation because they can't breathe. So, they can be seen coming to the surface to breathe. Since they need to eat in the water, they take in water and expel it through their blowholes, just as fish expel water through their gills. The blowhole is placed in front of the brain, where it releases the water without touching any of the blood-filled organs.

Mollusks and crustaceans, like crabs, also take in water for the same reason. These animals don't need cooling because they don't have much heat and are bloodless. The surrounding water cools them enough. But when they eat, they take in water, and they have to expel it to avoid swallowing it along with the food. Crustaceans, like crabs and lobsters, expel water through the folds beside their hairy parts, while cuttlefish and octopuses use the hollow above their heads. There's a more detailed explanation of these animals in *The History of Animals*.

This explains why animals take in water for cooling and how those that live in water must eat in it as well.

We must now explain how cooling happens in animals that breathe and those with gills. We've already said that all animals with lungs breathe. The reason some creatures have lungs, and those that do need to breathe, is that higher animals have more heat. Since they have a higher soul and nature than plants, they need this. Animals with more blood and warmth in their lungs tend to be larger, and the animal with the purest and most abundant blood in the lungs is the most upright—this is man. The reason man alone stands with his upper part directed toward the upper part of the universe is that he has such lungs.

So, the lungs must be considered an essential part of the animal's nature, both in humans and in other animals.

This is the purpose of cooling. As for the cause behind this, we must believe that nature made animals this way, just as it made many other animals with different compositions. Some animals have more earth in their makeup, like plants, while others, like aquatic animals, have more water. Winged and land animals have more air and fire, respectively. Each thing exists in the region that suits the element most abundant in its composition.

Empedocles was wrong when he said that animals with the most warmth and fire live in water to balance the heat in their bodies. He thought that since they lack cold and fluid, living in water keeps them alive, as water has less heat than air. But it makes no sense that water animals would all originate on land and then move to the water, especially since most of them have no legs. Yet, he said that they were first created on land and then moved to the water. But it's clear that water animals aren't warmer than land animals, as some have no blood at all, and others have very little.

We've already discussed what kinds of animals should be considered warm and what kinds cold. While

Empedocles' idea has some logic, his explanation is wrong. A condition that is too extreme is balanced by its opposite, but the best way for an animal's body to stay healthy is to be in an environment similar to its own nature. There's a difference between what an animal is made of and the condition of that material. For example, if nature made something out of wax or ice, it wouldn't be kept safe in a hot place because heat would quickly destroy it, as heat melts what cold freezes. Likewise, something made of salt or nitre wouldn't be placed in water because water would dissolve it, as its structure depends on being dry and warm.

So, if all bodies are made of wet and dry materials, it makes sense that things made mostly of wet and cold elements would live in liquid environments. And if they are cold, they would exist in cold places, while things made mostly of dry elements would be found on land. Trees, for instance, don't grow in water but on dry land. But according to Empedocles' theory, they should live in water because they are so dry, just like things that are very fiery. They would move to water, not because of the cold, but because of its fluid nature.

In reality, the natural state of materials is suited to the regions they exist in. Liquids belong in liquid environments, dry things on land, and warm things in the air. However, in terms of a body's condition, a cold environment helps balance out too much heat, while a warm one helps balance too much cold. The region around the animal adjusts the excess condition in its body. The regions where things live and the changing seasons also help fix such imbalances. But while a body's condition can be the opposite of its surroundings, the material that makes up the body cannot be. This explains why some animals are aquatic and others are terrestrial, and why some have lungs while others do not. It's not because of the amount of heat in their bodies, as Empedocles claimed.

The reason animals with lungs, especially those with lungs full of blood, breathe air is because the lungs are spongy and full of tubes. The lungs also have more blood than any other organ. All animals with blood-filled lungs need to cool down quickly because they don't have much room for changes in their body heat. The air needs to get through the entire lung because of the large amount of blood and heat it holds. Air can easily do this because it's light and can spread everywhere quickly, allowing it to cool down the body. Water, on the other hand, can't do this as easily.

This explains why animals with blood-filled lungs breathe more often—the more heat they have, the more cooling they need. Also, air can easily reach the source of heat in the heart.

To understand how the heart connects to the lungs through passages, we should look at dissections and the information in the *History of Animals*. The main reason animals need cooling is that the soul and fire come together in the heart. Breathing is how animals with lungs and a heart cool themselves. But for animals like fish, which live in water and don't have lungs, cooling happens through the gills using water. If you want to see how the heart connects to the gills, you need to look at dissections, and for more details, refer to *Natural History*. For now, we can sum it up like this.

It might seem like the heart is in a different position in land animals and fish, but the position is actually the same. The tip of the heart points in the direction the animal tilts its head. In fish, the tip of the heart points toward the mouth, since they don't tilt their heads the same way land animals do. From the tip of the heart, a large, strong tube runs to the center where all the gills meet. This is the biggest tube, but there are others on either side of the heart that go to each gill. Water constantly flows through the gills, cooling the heart.

In the same way fish move their gills, animals that breathe raise and lower their chest as they inhale and exhale. If there isn't enough fresh air, or if the air isn't replaced, they suffocate because the air, after touching the blood, heats up quickly. The heat from the blood cancels out the cooling effect, and when animals can't move their lungs (or fish can't move their gills) due to sickness or old age, they die.

Being born and dying are common to all animals, but there are different ways these things happen. There are different types of death, though they all have something in common. There is violent death, caused by something outside the body, and natural death, caused by something inside the body, built into the way the body is made. It's not something that comes from outside. For plants, this is called withering; for animals, it's called aging. Death and decay happen to everything that is fully developed, though it can also happen to things that aren't fully developed, like eggs or seeds before they sprout roots.

Death always happens due to a loss of heat, and in fully developed creatures, this happens when heat runs out in the organ that is the source of the creature's essential life. As we've said, this organ is located between the upper and lower parts of the body. In plants, it's between the root and the stem, and in animals with blood, it's the heart. In bloodless animals, it's the equivalent part of their body. Some animals have many potential sources of life, though they actually have only one. This explains why some insects can keep living even when they are cut in half, and why even some animals with blood can live for a long time after their heart is removed. For example, tortoises can still move their legs as long as they have their shell, which is due to their naturally weaker constitution, as we see in insects too.

Life ends when the heat that sustains it is no longer cooled properly. As I've said before, the heat burns itself up. So, when the lungs in one type of animal, or the gills in another, dry out over time, they become hard and earthy, unable to move. They can't expand or contract anymore. Eventually, the fire goes out due to exhaustion.

This is why even a small disturbance can cause death in old age. There isn't much heat left because most of it has been used up over the long life. Any extra strain on the body can quickly extinguish what's left. It's like the heart contains a small, weak flame that can easily be put out by the slightest movement. This is why death in old age is painless—there's no need for a violent event to cause it, and the soul departs quietly without feeling anything. Diseases that harden the lungs, such as tumors or excess heat from fevers, speed up breathing because the lungs can't move much either up or down. When the lungs can't move at all, breathing stops, and death follows.

Being born is when an animal first shares in the life-giving soul through warmth, and life is the process of keeping this connection. Youth is the time when the organ for cooling grows, old age is when it starts to decay, and the time in between is the prime of life.

A violent death happens when the vital heat is put out or burns out (both can cause death), while natural death happens when the heat runs out over time and life ends. For plants, this is called withering; for animals, it's called dying. In old age, death is caused by the body's inability to keep cooling itself due to the passage of time. This is our explanation of birth, life, and death, and why they happen in animals.

It is clear why animals that breathe air suffocate in water, and why fish suffocate in air. For fish, water provides the cooling they need, while for animals that breathe air, the air does the same. When either is taken away by a change in their environment, the function is lost.

We must also explain why gills and lungs move the way they do, and how this movement allows air or water to come in and go out. Here's how these organs are structured.

There are three things related to the heart that might seem similar but are actually different: palpitation, pulsation, and respiration.

Palpitation happens when the hot substance in the heart rushes together due to the cooling effect of waste products. This happens in conditions like spasms and other illnesses. It also occurs when you're scared, because when you're afraid, the upper parts of your body become cold, and the hot substance retreats to the heart. This causes the heart to palpitate because the heat is squeezed into such a small space that sometimes life is extinguished, and animals can die from fear and the disturbance it causes.

The constant beating of the heart is similar to the throbbing of an abscess. However, an abscess is painful because the blood changes in an unnatural way, and the throbbing continues until the matter inside is discharged. This process is similar to boiling, where heat turns liquid into vapor and expands it. But in an abscess, if nothing evaporates, the liquid thickens, and the process ends in the formation of pus. In boiling, it ends with the liquid escaping from the container.

In the heart, the beating is caused by heat expanding the liquid, which comes from food. This happens when the liquid rises to the outer wall of the heart and continues without stopping. There is always a constant flow of liquid that turns into blood, and the heart is where blood is first formed. We can see this in the early stages of life, as the heart contains blood before the veins become clear. This is why young people have faster pulses than older people, as there's more vapor being produced in the young.

All veins pulse at the same time because they are connected to the heart. Since the heart always beats, the veins also beat continuously and in sync with the heart.

So, palpitation is the heart's reaction to being squeezed by cold, while pulsation is caused by the heated liquid turning into vapor.

Respiration happens when the hot substance, which is the source of nutrition, grows. This part of the body needs more nutrition than other parts because it feeds them. As it grows, it makes the organ expand. This organ is built like a pair of bellows, similar to those used by blacksmiths. The heart and lungs have a similar shape. This structure must be double because the source of nutrition needs to be at the center of the natural forces.

As the organ expands, it causes the surrounding parts to rise. We can see this happen when people breathe. They lift their chest because the part inside the chest expands the same way. When this part expands, air rushes in like it would in bellows. The air is cold, so it cools the heat by reducing the excess fire. When the organ shrinks, the air that entered is pushed back out. When air enters, it's cold, but when it exits, it's warm because it has been in contact with the heat in the organ. This is especially true for animals with lungs full of blood. The lung has many tubes with blood vessels next to them, so it seems like the whole lung is full of blood. The movement of air inward is called respiration, and the movement outward is called expiration. This process continues for as long as the animal lives, as the organ keeps moving constantly. Life is tied to this constant movement of air in and out.

The movement of gills in fish happens in the same way. When the hot substance in the blood rises, the gills rise too and let water pass through. When the heat is cooled and flows back to the heart, the gills contract and push the water out. As the heat in the heart rises and then cools, this process repeats. So, just as breathing is tied to life and death in air-breathing animals, water entering and exiting is tied to life and death in fish.

We have now covered life, death, and related topics. But health and disease also deserve the attention of scientists, not just doctors, when it comes to understanding their causes. It's important to recognize the difference between the work of scientists and that of physicians, although they overlap in some ways. Doctors who are well-educated often mention natural science and claim that their methods come from it. On the other hand, the best scientists often take their studies so far that they end up discussing medical principles too.

• • •

The End

Thank you for Reading

Dear Reader,

We hope this timeless classic has sparked your imagination and enriched your literary journey. Now that you've turned the final page, we want to share a vision for the future of reading—one where every classic you've ever wanted to explore is at your fingertips, in a format that best suits your life.

We'd like to invite you to **gain immediate, unlimited digital & audiobook access** to hundreds of the most treasured literary classics ever written—along with the option to **secure deluxe paperback, hardcover & box set editions at printing cost**. Together, we can **spark a new global literary renaissance** alongside our small, independent publishing house called "The Library of Alexandria."

Thousands of years ago, the Library of Alexandria stood as a beacon of knowledge—until it was lost to history. We aim to reignite that spirit of preservation and discovery right now, in the modern age—only this time, it's accessible to all, in every language and every format.

Picture a world where every timeless classic, novel, poem, or philosophical treatise is not only available to read but also updated for today's readers—modernized, translated into any language or dialect, and ready to enjoy in any format you choose, whether that is in an eBook, audiobook, paperback, or deluxe hardcover & box set version a printing cost.

By joining our movement to **rebuild the modern Library of Alexandria,** you become part of an unprecedented mission to offer:

- **Unlimited Audiobook & eBook Access to the Greatest Classics of All Time**

    Instantly explore thousands of legendary works, from Plato and Shakespeare to Jane Austen and Leo Tolstoy. All are instantly ready to read or listen to, giving you a complete literary universe at your fingertips.

- **Paperback & Deluxe Editions at Printing Costs:**
    Purchase any title in a paperback, deluxe hardbound, or deluxe boxset edition at printing costs, shipped right to your doorstep. Curate your personal library of Alexandria with editions worthy of display—crafted to last, designed to captivate, and delivered straight to your door.

- **Modern translations for Contemporary Readers in all languages and dialects**

Discover a vast selection of classics reimagined in clear, current language—no more struggling with outdated phrases or obscure references. Next to the original versions, we aim to offer translations in as many languages and dialects as possible.

As we continue our translation efforts and add new languages, readers everywhere can connect with these works as if they were written today. *By bridging linguistic divides, you're contributing to ensuring that these timeless stories become more meaningful, accessible, and inspiring for people across the globe.*

- **Your Personal Library of Alexandria:**

  Over the months and years, you'll curate a unique physical archive of classics—each volume a testament to your taste, curiosity, and love of knowledge. It's not just about owning books—it's about curating a cultural legacy you'll cherish and pass down for generations to come.

- **Join a Global Literary Renaissance:**

  Your support fuels an ongoing mission: allowing us to reinvest in offering deluxe print editions (including special boxsets) at their true cost, broaden the range of available formats and translations, and extend the reach of these works to new audiences worldwide.

By joining today, you're not just preserving a legacy of masterpieces; *you set in motion a powerful wave of literary accessibility.*

We are more than a publisher—we're a movement, and we can't do it alone. Your support lets us scale our mission, preserving and reimagining history's greatest works for tomorrow's readers.

Become a Torchbearer of knowledge.

Thank you for picking up this book and allowing us into your literary journey. As you turn the pages, know that you're part of something larger: a global effort to keep these stories alive, share their wisdom across borders and generations, and spark a true cultural revival for the modern era.

If this resonates with you—please consider taking the next step. By visiting:
www.libraryofalexandria.com

With gratitude and a shared love of knowledge,

The Modern Library of Alexandria Team

Visit:

www.libraryofalexandria.com

Or scan the code below:

www.ingramcontent.com/pod-product-compliance
Lightning Source LLC
Chambersburg PA
CBHW012012290326
41934CB00017BA/3469